Russian Rigging

Russian Rigging

The Evidence The Election Was Hacked

Mark Shilling

Acknowledgements

CNN, whose dedication to priming, framing and agenda-setting made this work necessary.

Stefan Molyneux, whose thorough compilation of evidence and reasoned arguments formed the core of this work.

Cici, who provided the inspiration for this work.

Contents

Chapter I

The Evidence

November 8th, 2016

November 9th, 2016

November 10th, 2016

November 11th, 2016

November 12th, 2016

November 13th, 2016

November 14th, 2016

November 15th, 2016

November 16th, 2016

November 17th, 2016

November 18th, 2016

November 19th, 2016

November 20th, 2016

November 21st, 2016

November 22nd, 2016

November 23rd, 2016

November 24th, 2016

November 25th, 2016

November 26th, 2016

November 27th, 2016

November 28th, 2016

November 29th, 2016

November 30th, 2016

December 1st, 2016

December 2nd, 2016

December 3rd, 2016

December 4th, 2016

December 5th, 2016

December 6th, 2016

December 7th, 2016

December 8th, 2016

December 9th, 2016

December 10th, 2016

December 11th, 2016

December 12th, 2016

December 13th, 2016

December 14th, 2016

December 15th, 2016

December 16th, 2016

December 17th, 2016

December 18th, 2016

December 19th, 2016

December 20th, 2016

December 21st, 2016

December 22nd, 2016

December 23rd, 2016

December 24th, 2016

December 25th, 2016

December 26th, 2016

December 27th, 2016

December 28th, 2016

December 29th, 2016

December 30th, 2016

December 31st, 2016

January 1st, 2017

January 2nd, 2017

January 3rd, 2017

January 4th, 2017

January 5th, 2017

January 6th, 2017

January 7th, 2017

January 8th, 2017

January 9th, 2017

January 10th, 2017

January 11th, 2017

January 12th, 2017

January 13th, 2017

January 14th, 2017

January 15th, 2017

January 16th, 2017

January 17th, 2017

January 18th, 2017

January 19th, 2017

January 20th, 2017

January 21st, 2017

January 22nd, 2017

January 23rd, 2017

January 24th, 2017

January 25th, 2017

January 26th, 2017

January 27th, 2017

January 28th, 2017

January 29th, 2017

January 30th, 2017

January 31st, 2017

February 1st, 2017

February 2nd, 2017

February 3rd, 2017

February 4th, 2017

February 5th, 2017

February 6th, 2017

February 7th, 2017

February 8th, 2017

February 9th, 2017

February 10th, 2017

February 11th, 2017

February 12th, 2017

February 13th, 2017

February 14th, 2017

February 15th, 2017

February 16th, 2017

February 17th, 2017

February 18th, 2017

February 19th, 2017

February 20th, 2017

February 21st, 2017

February 22nd, 2017

February 23rd, 2017

February 24th, 2017

February 25th, 2017

February 26th, 2017

February 27th, 2017

February 28th, 2017

March 1st, 2017

March 2nd, 2017

March 3rd, 2017

March 4th, 2017

March 5th, 2017

March 6th, 2017

March 7th, 2017

March 8th, 2017

March 9th, 2017

March 10th, 2017

March 11th, 2017

March 12th, 2017

March 13th, 2017

March 14th, 2017

March 15th, 2017

March 16th, 2017

March 17th, 2017

March 18th, 2017

March 19th, 2017

March 20th, 2017

March 21st, 2017

March 22nd, 2017

March 23rd, 2017

March 24th, 2017

March 25th, 2017

March 26th, 2017

March 27th, 2017

March 28th, 2017

March 29th, 2017

March 30th, 2017

March 31st, 2017

April 1st, 2017

April 2nd, 2017

April 3rd, 2017

April 4th, 2017

April 5th, 2017

April 6th, 2017

Appendix

Glossary

Bibliography

Index